# THE ULTIMATE *Otter* BOOK

JENNY KELLETT

The Ultimate Otter Book

Cover and Book Design: Jenny Kellett

**Sign up for our VIP Club:**
www.bellanovabooks.com/newsletter



ISBN: 978-2-487191-00-6
Imprint: Bellanova Books

# CONTENTS

Are you ready to plunge into the enchanting world of otters? These playful creatures, known for their charming antics and graceful swimming, have so much more to them than meets the eye.

On this journey, you'll uncover fascinating facts about different otter species from around the world. Ever wondered how an otter's sleek fur keeps them warm? Or how they communicate with each other in their tight-knit families? We've got all those answers and more!

## WHAT ARE OTTERS?

Let's start with the basics! These playful and adorable animals can be found in rivers, lakes, and oceans all around the world! Otters are part of a group of animals called **mustelids**, which means they are related to weasels, ferrets, and badgers. Despite their cuddly appearance, otters are skilled predators, which means they are excellent at catching their food.

**A group of otters is called a romp or a raft.**

## DIFFERENT SPECIES OF OTTERS

There are 13 different species of otters, and each one has its own unique features and personality. From the small-clawed otter of Asia, which is the smallest species, to the giant otter of South America, which can grow up to 6 feet long, otters come in all shapes and sizes. We will look at the different species in more detail in the first chapter.

## WHERE DO OTTERS LIVE?

Otters are world travelers! You can find them on every continent except Australia and Antarctica. Whether it's the cold oceans of Alaska, where sea otters float, or the freshwater rivers of Africa, where you might spot a spotted-necked otter, these animals have adapted to a variety of environments.

By the end of this journey, not only will you be brimming with knowledge about otters, but you'll also be inspired to play your part in protecting these wonderful creatures and the beautiful environments they call home.

So, are you ready to slide into this adventure? Let's make a splash and get started!

# OTTERLY DIFFERENT SPECIES

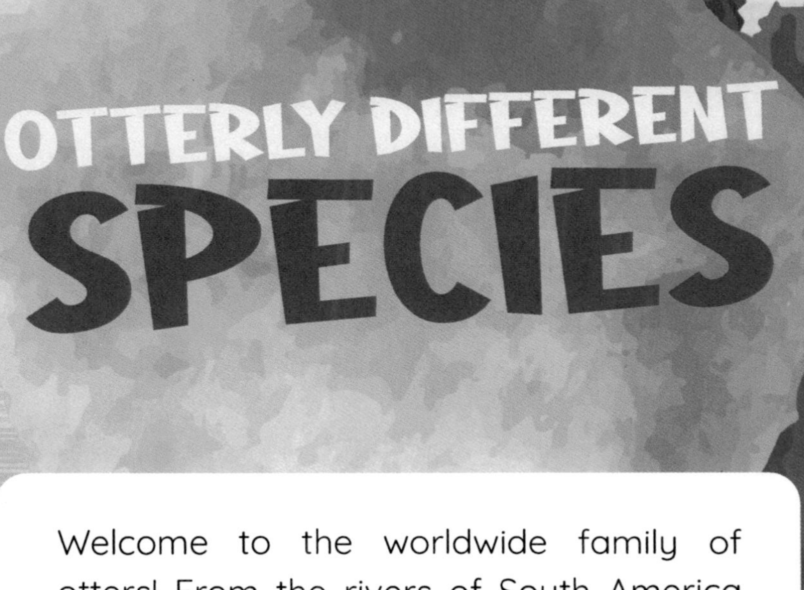

Welcome to the worldwide family of otters! From the rivers of South America to the coasts of Japan, otters have made homes in all kinds of waterways. Let's dive into the 13 different species of otters and explore what makes each one, and their environments, unique.

# ASIAN OTTERS

## EURASIAN OTTER

(Scientific name: *Lutra lutra*)

**Where they live:** Europe, Asia, and North Africa.

**Characteristics:** Also known as the Eurasian river otter, these otters boast sleek brown fur and long, muscular tails. Their diet consists mainly of fish, but they won't say no to amphibians!

**Fun Fact:** They have a huge territory, sometimes traveling up to 25 miles to find food!

# ASIAN SMALL-CLAWED OTTER

## (Scientific name: *Aonyx cinereus)*

**Where They Live:** Southeast Asia and parts of southern China.

**Characteristics:** The smallest otter species, they have distinctively short claws and webbed fingers. Found in Southeast Asia's mangroves and freshwater wetlands, they're vocal and extremely sociable.

**Fun Fact:** They are the most social of all otter species and are often seen in large family groups.

## SMOOTH-COATED OTTER

(Scientific name: *Lutrogale perspicillata*)

**Where They Live:** South Asia, from India to Southeast Asia.

**Characteristics:** As their name suggests, they have a smoother and shorter coat than other otters, which comes in handy in their aquatic environment.

**Fun Fact:** They are known to “sing” when they are out and about, exploring their territory.

## HAIRY-NOSED OTTER

**(Scientific name:** ***Lutra sumatrana*****)**

**Where They Live:** Southeast Asia

**Characteristics:** One of the rarest otter species, these Southeast Asian natives have distinct hairy noses. Living in forested and coastal areas, they are elusive and primarily feed on fish.

**Fun Fact:** They were once thought to be extinct but were rediscovered in the wild in 1998!

# AFRICAN OTTERS

## SPOTTED-NECKED OTTER

(Scientific name: *Hydrictis maculicollis*)

**Where They Live:** Lakes and rivers in sub-Saharan Africa.

**Characteristics:** They have unique, spotted fur on their neck and chest.

**Fun Fact:** They are excellent divers and catch most of their food underwater.

Image: Marc Henrion

## AFRICAN CLAWLESS OTTER

(Scientific name: *Aonyx capensis*)

**Where They Live:** Sub-Saharan Africa

**Characteristics:** Unlike other otters, they have no claws, just dexterous fingers for finding food under rocks. They prefer slower-moving waters and have a taste for crabs and fish.

**Fun Fact:** They are the third largest species of otter, after the giant otter and sea otter.

Image: Mark Paxton of Shamvura Camp, Namibia

## CONGO CLAWLESS OTTER

(Scientific name: *Aonyx congicus)*

**Where They Live:** Central African swamps and rivers, particularly around the Congo River.

**Characteristics:** Similar to the African clawless otter but smaller and with a lighter throat patch. They have smooth, dense fur that is usually brown or grayish-brown. They are a medium-sized otter, typically reach lengths of up to about 1.3 meters (around 4 feet) from nose to tail tip.

**Fun Fact:** They are the least studied of all otter species due to their remote habitat.

Image copyright Rita Chapman

# AMERICAN OTTERS

## NEOTROPICAL OTTER

(Scientific name: *Lontra longicaudis*)

**Where They Live:** Rivers, lakes, and wetlands in Central and South America.

**Characteristics:** Solitary and territorial, they have a more slender body and longer tail.

**Fun Fact:** They are great climbers and often perch in trees to watch their surroundings.

# NORTH AMERICAN RIVER OTTER

**(Scientific name: *Lontra canadensis*)**

**Where They Live:** North America, in rivers, lakes, and estuaries.

**Characteristics:** Playful and social, they often slide down muddy or snowy banks just for fun. They have dense fur for insulation and are great swimmers.

Image: Dmitry Azovtsev

**Fun Fact:** They can stay underwater for up to 8 minutes!

## GIANT OTTER

**(Scientific name: *Pteronura brasiliensis*)**

**Where They Live:** Rivers and lakes in South America.

**Characteristics:** As the largest otter species, they can grow up to 6 feet long!

**Fun Fact:** They are known as the “river wolf” and have a unique throat pattern that is different on each otter, like a human fingerprint.

## SOUTHERN RIVER OTTER

(Scientific name: *Lontra provocax)*

**Where They Live:** Freshwater and marine habitats in Chile and Argentina.

**Characteristics:** One of the rarest otter species, they have a short, dense coat of fur.

**Fun Fact:** They are very secretive and prefer to stay hidden from humans.

Image: Kevin Schafer

## SEA OTTER

**(Scientific name: *Enhydra lutris*)**

**Where They Live:** Coastal areas in the North Pacific Ocean.

**Characteristics:** Larger than most otters, they have incredibly dense fur and often float on their backs.

**Fun Fact:** They use rocks as tools to crack open hard shells of their prey, like clams and urchins.

## MARINE OTTER

**(Scientific name:** ***Lontra felina*****)**

**Where They Live:** Coastal areas of southern Chile and Argentina.

**Characteristics:** Despite their name, they aren't as adapted to marine life as sea otters and often stay close to shore. Sadly, they are endangered.

**Fun Fact:** They are also called "sea cats" because of their unique, more cat-like face.

Ever wonder how otters make such a splash in the water? Let's dive deeper into the incredible features and adaptations that make otters the water-loving creatures they are!

Otters are a testament to nature's ingenuity. Every part of their body, from their streamlined shape to their sensory whiskers, is fine-tuned for life in aquatic environments. Their adaptations aren't just about survival—they're about thriving, playing, and enjoying their watery homes to the fullest.

# BODY STRUCTURE

Otters are built for water! Their slender, elongated bodies minimize resistance, allowing them to move smoothly and quickly. Their necks are almost as wide as their heads, letting them twist and turn to catch slippery prey. And don't forget their strong tails! Acting like rudders on a boat, these muscular tails provide speed and direction, essential for chasing after quick fish or escaping predators.

**While an otter's legs might seem short, their powerful muscles give them a surprising burst of speed, both in water and on land.**

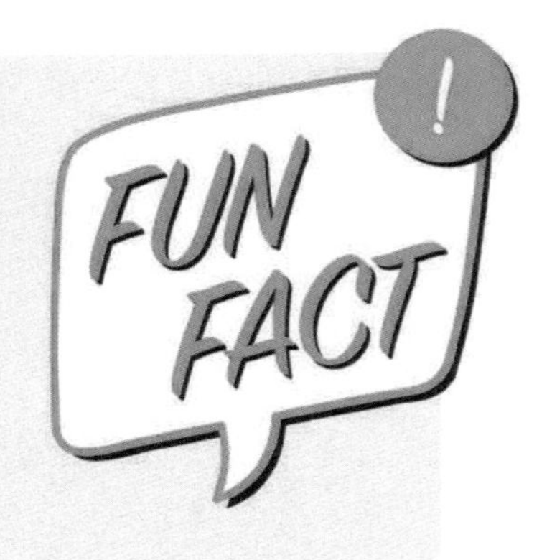

# FUR & INSULATION

Let's talk about the otter's fabulous coat! This isn't just any fur—it's a lifesaver in chilly waters. The soft underfur traps air, creating a warm layer next to their skin. The longer, outer guard hairs are waterproof and keep the underfur dry. Otters also have special sebaceous glands that produce oil, which they spread throughout their fur by grooming, enhancing its waterproof properties.

# WEBBED FEET

Otters have a special feature on their feet—webbing! This skin between their toes turns their feet into powerful flippers. The webbing provides a larger surface area, making each stroke in the water more efficient. It's like they're wearing built-in flippers!

Otters also have claws, which aren't just used for defense. They also help in grasping slippery prey like fish and crustaceans. Although, as you already know—not all otters have claws.

**Otters spend a lot of their day grooming! This not only keeps their fur clean but also ensures it stays waterproof and insulated.**

# WHISKERS AND SENSES

An otter's world is full of sensory wonders, and their whiskers play a starring role! These long, sensitive whiskers, known as **vibrissae**, can detect tiny vibrations in the water, alerting them to nearby prey or danger. When visibility is low, they rely heavily on this whisker "sixth sense." Additionally, otters have keen eyesight, especially underwater, and their ears close up tight when diving, to keep water out.

**Otters have a special membrane over their eyes, like built-in goggles, which protects them and gives clear vision underwater.**

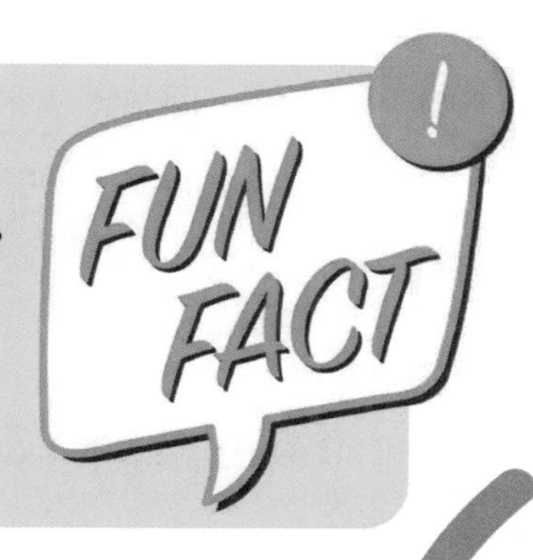

# HUNTING & DIET

Otters aren't just playful creatures; they're also skilled hunters with a diverse palate. The dining habits of otters provide us with a fascinating look into nature's balance.

Let's explore what's on an otter's menu and how they play a significant role in their ecosystems.

## What Otters Eat: From Fish to Frogs

An otter's diet is vast and varies depending on where they live and the species of otter. A common favorite? Fish! Fresh, slippery, and nutritious, fish makes up a significant part of many otters' diets. But otters don't stop there. They munch on:

- **Crustaceans:** Think crabs, crayfish, and shrimp.
- **Amphibians:** Like juicy frogs and salamanders.
- **Mollusks:** Snails and clams are on the menu too.
- **Birds and Small Mammals:** Occasionally, some otters will snack on these, especially if other food sources are scarce.

Fun Fact
An otter's metabolism is so high that they need to eat about 15-25% of their body weight every day to stay energized!

## Hunting Techniques and Tools

Otters are not just good hunters; they're ingenious ones! Depending on what they're after, they might:

- **Dive Deep:** Sea otters can dive up to 80 feet in search of prey (river otters typically dive between 20-30 feet), using their sharp eyesight and sensitive whiskers to detect food.
- **Use Tools:** Particularly sea otters, which often use rocks to crack open hard-shelled prey.
- **Swift Pursuit:** Using their streamlined bodies and powerful tails, they chase down faster prey like fish.
- **Forage:** Poking around i[illegible] underwater crevices [illegible] digging in the mud can yi[illegible] invertebrates.

THE
OTTER
LIFESTYLE

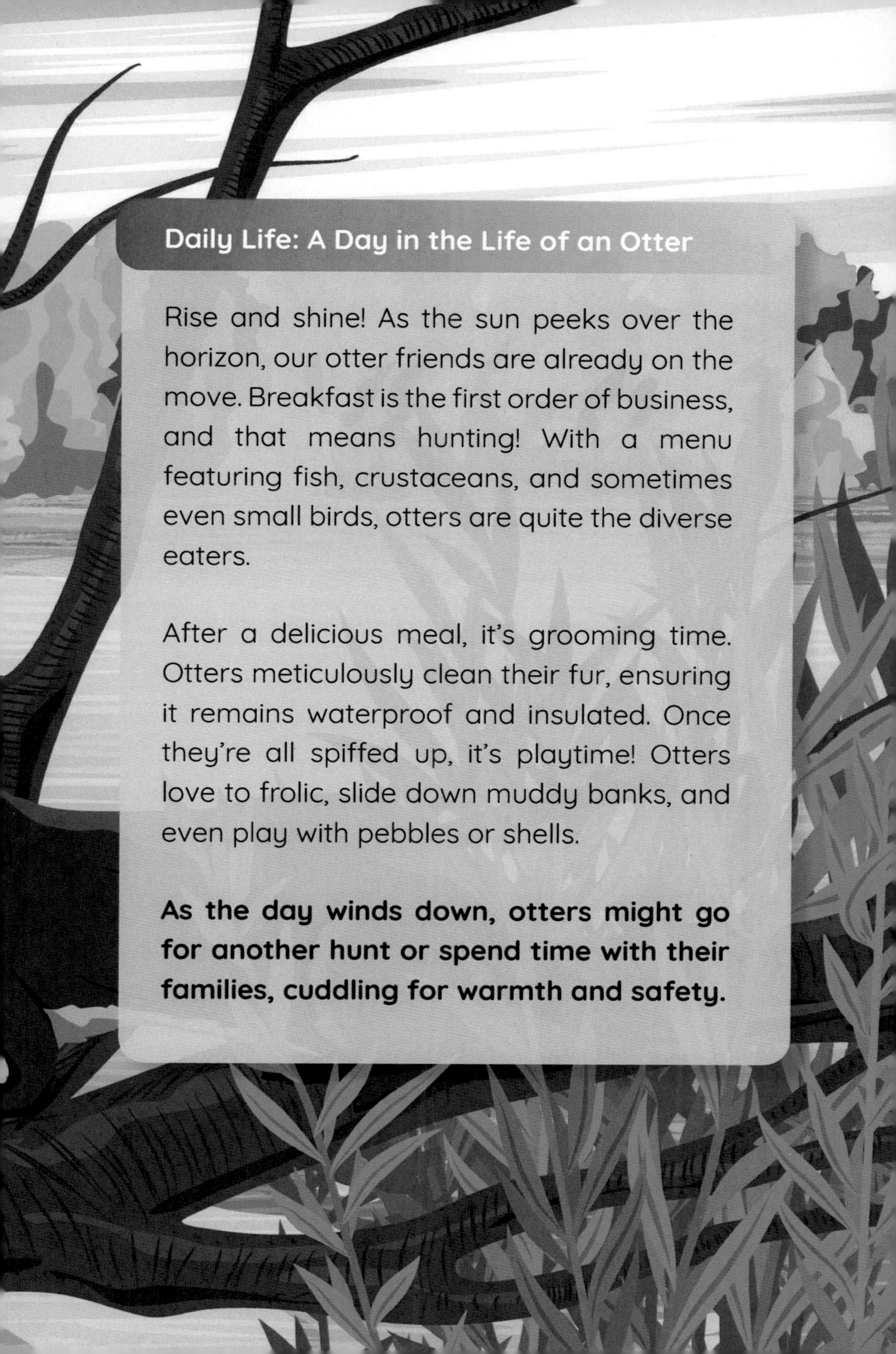

## Daily Life: A Day in the Life of an Otter

Rise and shine! As the sun peeks over the horizon, our otter friends are already on the move. Breakfast is the first order of business, and that means hunting! With a menu featuring fish, crustaceans, and sometimes even small birds, otters are quite the diverse eaters.

After a delicious meal, it's grooming time. Otters meticulously clean their fur, ensuring it remains waterproof and insulated. Once they're all spiffed up, it's playtime! Otters love to frolic, slide down muddy banks, and even play with pebbles or shells.

**As the day winds down, otters might go for another hunt or spend time with their families, cuddling for warmth and safety.**

## SOCIAL STRUCTURES: FAMILY AND GROUP DYNAMICS

Family is everything for otters! Many species, like the river otter, have strong family bonds, with parents teaching their young essential life skills. Sea otters, on the other hand, often have a more solitary lifestyle.

But, there's one thing many otters have in common: the raft. When they're not busy with their daily routines, groups of sea otters sometimes float together in formations called rafts, holding hands to stay connected!

## COMMUNICATION: HOW OTTERS TALK TO EACH OTHER

Chirps, whistles, growls, and even purrs - otters have a wide range of vocalizations. These sounds help them communicate everything from warnings about nearby predators to expressing joy during playtime. Baby otters, called **pups**, have a special cry that their mothers quickly recognize.

But otters don't just communicate with sounds. They also use body language! A raised tail might indicate alarm, while playful wrestling is a sign of friendly bonding.

Otters have scent glands, which they use to mark their territory. By leaving these scented messages, they tell other otters about their presence.

# OTTERS AT PLAY

Watching otters play is one of nature's most delightful sights.

But have you ever wondered why they're so playful? Let's uncover the joy and purpose behind their fun-filled antics!

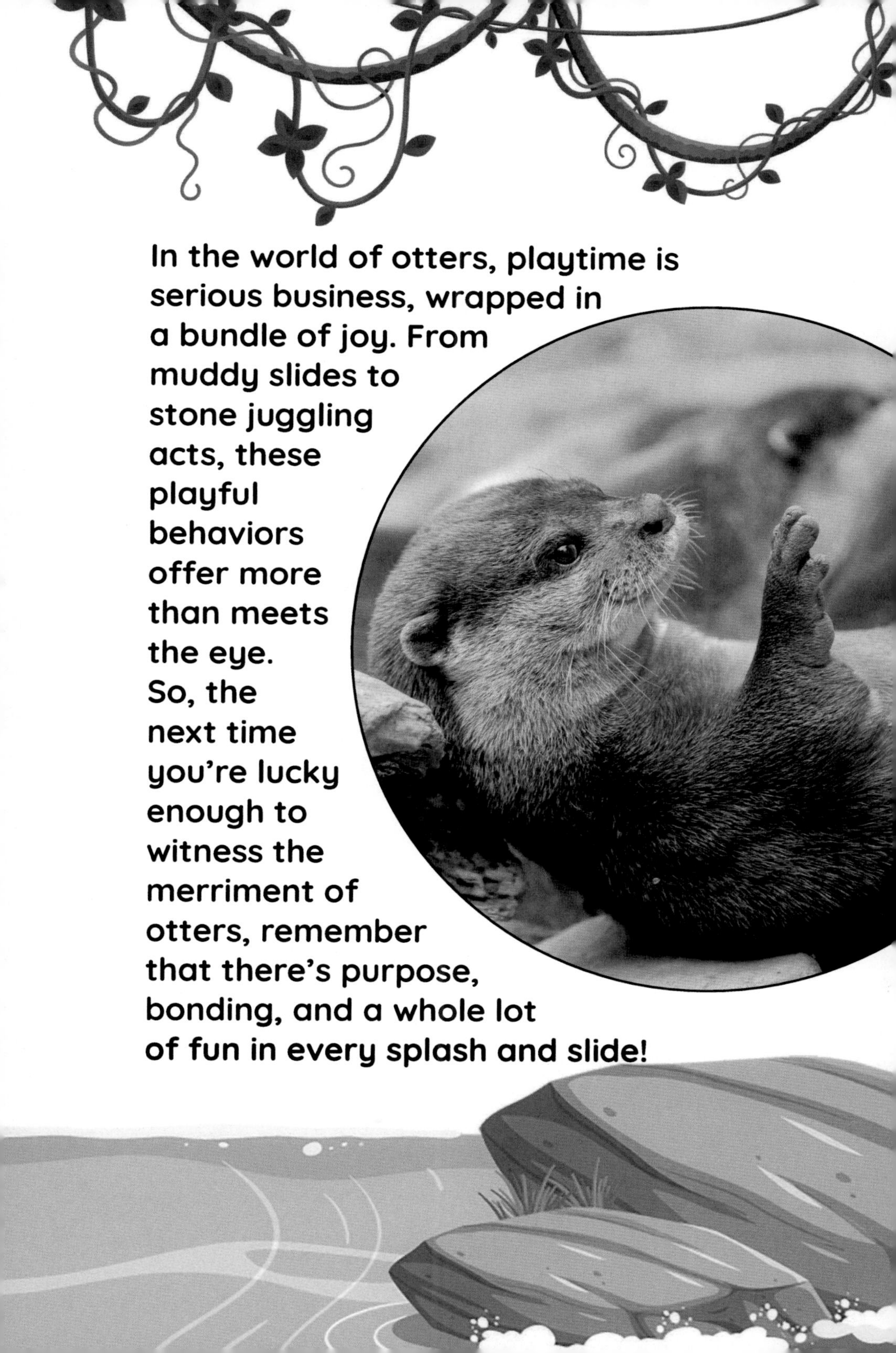

In the world of otters, playtime is serious business, wrapped in a bundle of joy. From muddy slides to stone juggling acts, these playful behaviors offer more than meets the eye. So, the next time you're lucky enough to witness the merriment of otters, remember that there's purpose, bonding, and a whole lot of fun in every splash and slide!

## Playful Behavior: Why Otters Love to Play

The playful behavior of otters isn't just about having a good time—there's a purpose behind the play! For otters, play is a way to practice essential survival skills. Sliding down banks, for example, helps young otters learn how to navigate their wetland habitats. Playing chase hones their hunting skills. So, when you see otters playing, remember, they're not just goofing around; they're in training!

## Fun & Games

- **WATER SLIDES:** Otters love a good slide! Using their belly as a sled, they'll slide down muddy or snowy riverbanks into the water.
- **STONE JUGGLING:** Especially common among sea otters, they'll often juggle small rocks, passing them between their paws and rolling them around on their chests.
- **WRESTLING:** Otters often engage in playful wrestling matches, darting and diving through the water.

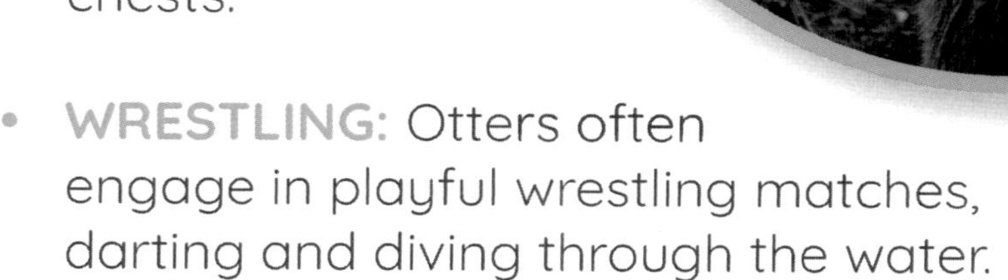

During play, otter pups learn the art of sharing, often passing toys or pebbles back and forth with their siblings.

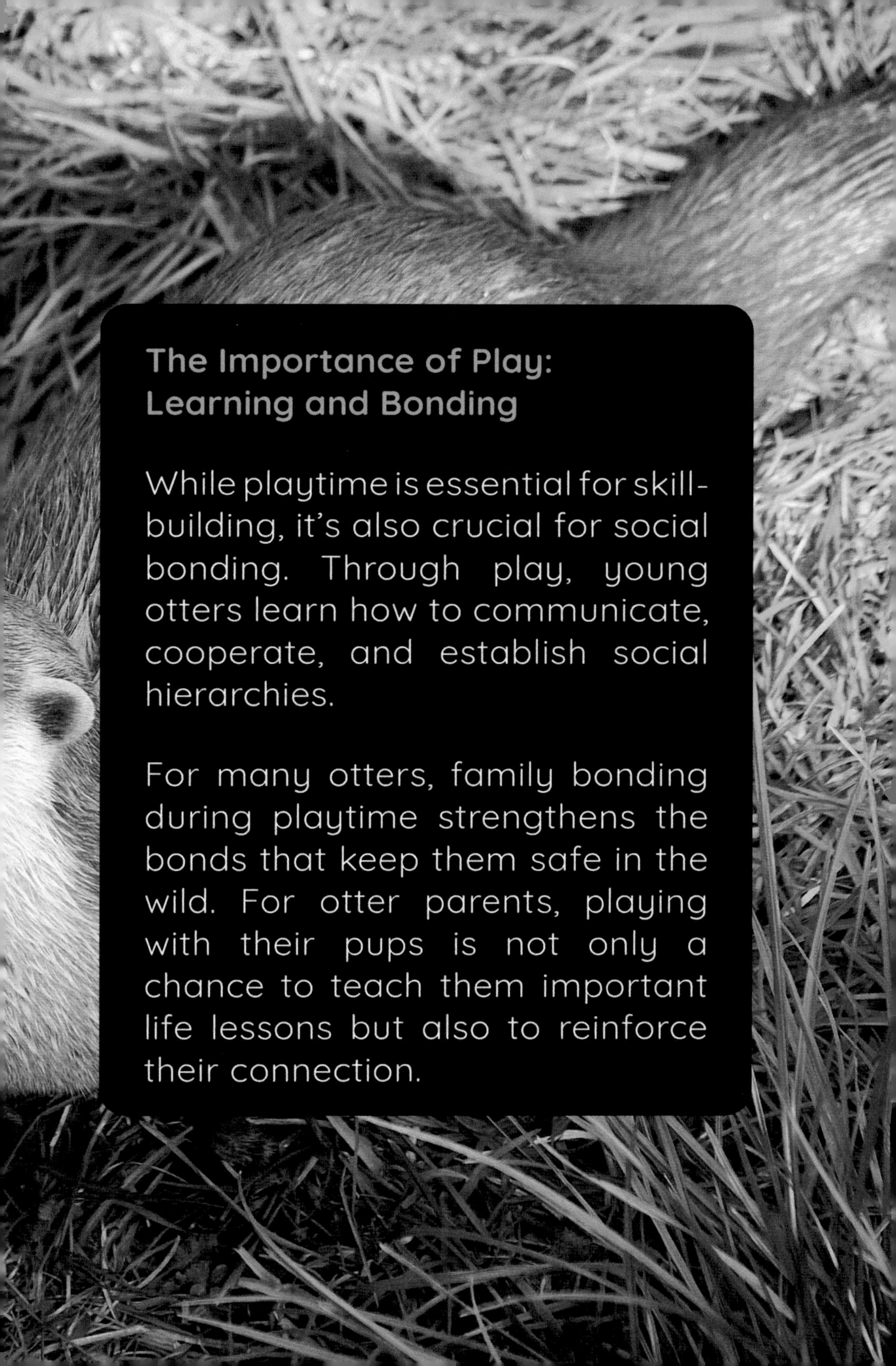

## The Importance of Play: Learning and Bonding

While playtime is essential for skill-building, it's also crucial for social bonding. Through play, young otters learn how to communicate, cooperate, and establish social hierarchies.

For many otters, family bonding during playtime strengthens the bonds that keep them safe in the wild. For otter parents, playing with their pups is not only a chance to teach them important life lessons but also to reinforce their connection.

# FROM BIRTH TO ADULTHOOD

Have you ever wondered what life is like for a baby otter? Let's take a peek into the first magical moments and the journey to adulthood for these furry bundles of joy.

Photographer Michael Baird captured this rare sight of a mother otter with twin pups in California! They are one or two days old.

## THE FIRST MOMENTS: OTTER PUPS

When otter pups come into the world, they are enveloped in a warm and nurturing environment, usually a cozy den built by their mother near the water. Born blind and toothless, these tiny creatures weigh only a fraction of their adult counterparts. Despite their vulnerability, they are far from helpless! Thanks to their fluffy fur, they are **buoyant**, meaning they naturally float—a lifesaver for a creature destined for an aquatic lifestyle.

Image: Tim Felce

## LIFE IN THE NURSERY DEN

During the first few weeks, the mother keeps a watchful eye on her pups, nursing them with her rich milk full of nutrients. Some otter moms, like those of the sea otter species, even wrap their babies in kelp to keep them anchored in one place while they go hunting! Talk about ingenious childcare!

## LEARNING THE ROPES: ADOLESCENCE

As they grow, the pups begin to learn crucial life skills, like swimming and grooming. Keeping their fur clean and well-maintained is essential for insulation and buoyancy. In some otter families, the father and older siblings join in on the teaching, helping the youngsters master the art of catching prey like fish and crustaceans. By observing and mimicking, pups learn the ropes, from swimming effortlessly to performing intricate dives and turns.

## TAKING THE LEAP: INTO ADULTHOOD

Around a year old, otters are ready to embark on their own adventures. They're now adept swimmers and hunters, equipped with all the skills they need for an independent life. For some species, like the Eurasian river otter, this is when they set out to establish their own territories. But for others, like the giant otter, family bonds remain strong, and they often stay in the same social groups for years.

## FAMILY TIES

But whether they choose to set off into the world or stick with their families, otters carry the teachings and bonds of their early years throughout their lifetimes. These lessons shape them into the agile, skilled, and sociable creatures we've come to love and admire.

# OTTERS IN DANGER

## The struggles of otters

Otters, with their playful antics and graceful swimming, have won our hearts. But, it's sad to know that these amazing animals face some pretty big challenges in the wild.

It's a tough time for otters, but with understanding, care, and action, we can make the world a safer place for them. And you, as an otter-lover, can help spread the word! Let's dive into what's troubling our otter friends and what's being done to help.

## POLLUTION

Imagine trying to swim with a plastic bag wrapped around you! Pollution, especially from plastic and chemicals, can hurt otters. They can get tangled in trash or get sick from polluted water.

## HABITAT LOSS

As forests are cut down and rivers are changed for human uses, otters lose their homes. Just like you need a safe place to sleep and play, otters need safe rivers and coastlines.

## HUNTING

In some parts of the world, otters are hunted for their beautiful fur. Thankfully, many countries have now made this illegal, but it still happens illegally.

## FARMING

Pesticides used in farming can end up in rivers and harm the fish. When otters eat these fish, they too can get sick!

## IT'S NOT ALL BAD NEWS!

There are many organizations and teams of scientists who are working super hard to protect otters.

They help by cleaning up rivers, creating safe spaces for otters, and teaching people all about why otters are so important.

These are just a few of the organizations that work hard to protect otters and other wildlife. Check out their websites and see how you can get involved!

People around the world are rolling up their sleeves to help otters thrive and dance once again in their aquatic playgrounds. And guess what? You can help too! Let's discover how you can become an otter hero.

## SUPPORT CONSERVATION ORGANIZATIONS

Help otters by supporting organizations that protect them, such as those on the previous page. Donate, adopt an otter, or purchase merchandise to help them.

**Idea:** *Ask for donations to an otter charity instead of gifts for your next birthday or holiday celebration.*

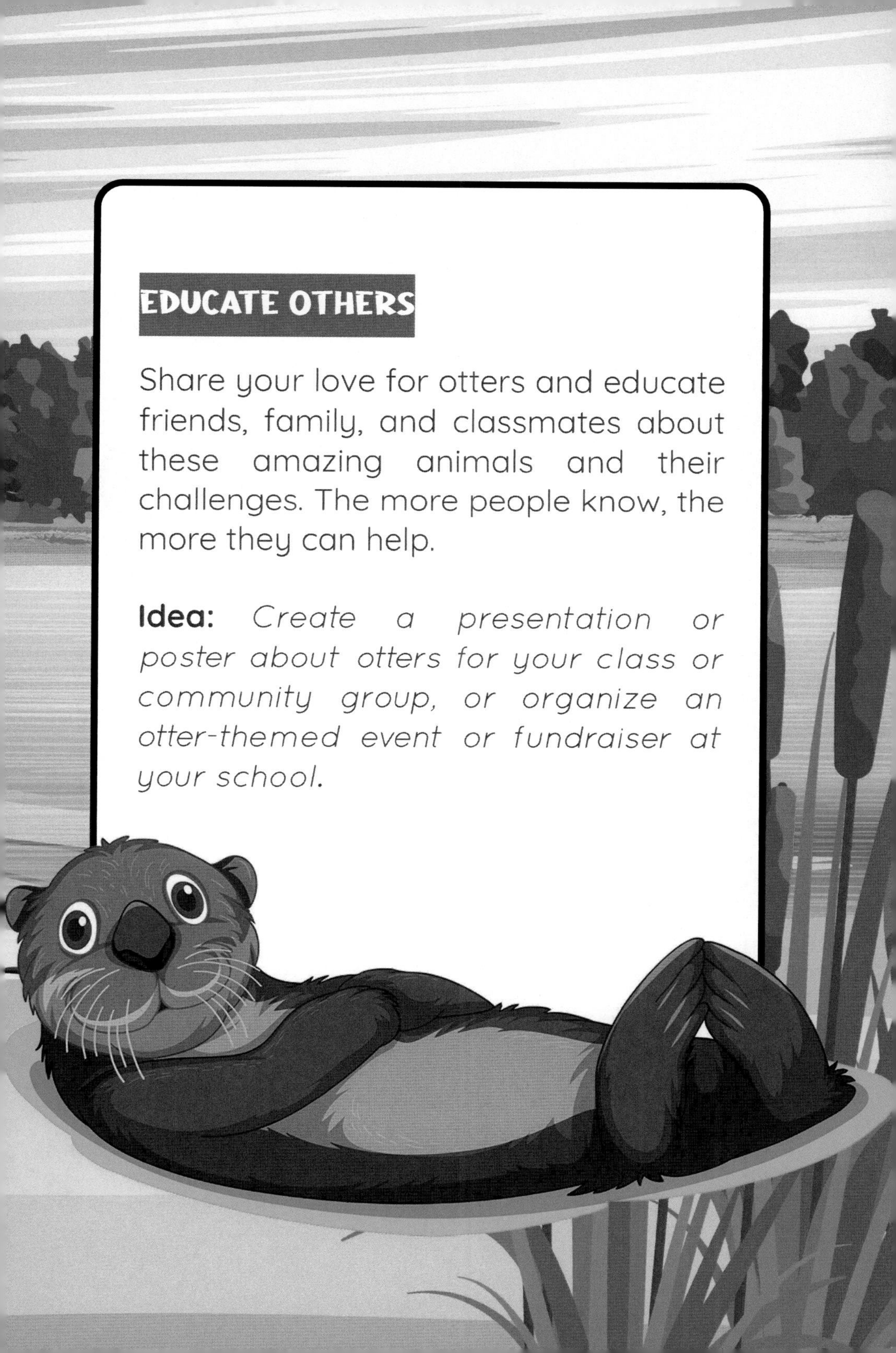

## EDUCATE OTHERS

Share your love for otters and educate friends, family, and classmates about these amazing animals and their challenges. The more people know, the more they can help.

**Idea:** *Create a presentation or poster about otters for your class or community group, or organize an otter-themed event or fundraiser at your school.*

## MAKE ENVIRONMENTALLY FRIENDLY CHOICES

Protect the environment and otter habitats by recycling, conserving water, and using energy-efficient appliances. Just by using less plastic you will make a big difference!

**Idea:** *Start a recycling program at your school or neighborhood or create a fun energy or water-saving challenge in your household.*

## CLEAN-UP CREW

It's super important to keep our rivers and oceans clean to make them safer for otters, and other creatures.

**Idea:** *Join or organize local clean-up days at nearby beaches, rivers, or lakes. Less trash means happier otters!.*

**From tiny ripples to big splashes, every action counts. By lending a hand (or paw!), we can make sure that otters continue to glide, play, and thrive in our wonderful world.**

**Together, we can make a brighter future for them!**

# OTTERS AND HUMANS

Otters and humans have shared countless moments together throughout history.

From stories passed down through generations to our relationships today, otters have splashed their way into our hearts. Let's discover more about this bond!

# OTTERS IN MYTHOLOGY AND FOLKLORE

From fairy tales to campfire stories, otters have been the stars of many a legend:

**ANCIENT EGYPT:** Did you know that the people of Ancient Egypt thought otters were extra special? They believed otters brought good luck, and sometimes they even made otter statues to keep by their side.

**NATIVE AMERICAN TALES:** Some Native American stories picture otters as cheeky, fun-loving characters. They believed otters had the power to make people smile and laugh.

**JAPANESE STORIES:** Japan has tales of "kawauso," river otters that can change into people! But these otters weren't scary; they just loved playing tricks and having fun. Right is a drawing depicting one of these stories.

## OTTERS AND LOCAL COMMUNITIES

Otters can sometimes cause a splash in the communities they live near, both in positive and challenging ways:

**FRIENDLY RIVALS:** In places like the fishing villages of Bintulu in Malaysia, otters are often seen nabbing fish right from the nets. While they might be viewed as competitors by the fisherfolk, they're just trying to grab a meal in their own clever way.

**TOURIST MAGNETS:** Morro Bay in California, USA, (*pictured behind*) is a popular spot for otter watching. Tourists flock there to watch the sea otters float on their backs, use tools, and play in the kelp forests. The local businesses, like cafes and souvenir shops, benefit from this otterly awesome attraction!

**OTTER DAY:** In Japan, there's a town called Iwate where locals celebrate an "Otter Day" to spread awareness about otter conservation and share knowledge about these amazing creatures.

## OTTERS AS PETS: THINK TWICE

Now, you might look at an otter's adorable face and playful behavior and think, "I wish I could have one at home!" But here's the thing: otters are wild animals, and they're happiest when they're in their natural environment. Here's why:

**SPECIAL NEEDS:** Otters need a lot of space, especially water, to roam and play. They eat a specific diet that can be hard to replicate at home. They aren't like cats or dogs; their needs are much more complex.

**IT'S THE LAW:** In many places, it's illegal to have otters as pets. These laws exist to protect both otters and people. Removing otters from the wild can also hurt their populations and the health of local ecosystems.

**NATURAL INSTINCTS:** In the wild, otters do things like dig, forage, and explore vast areas. At home, this might translate to digging up your sofa or chewing on things. It's not them being naughty; it's just them being otters!

**REMEMBER!** Otters may look cute and playful, but they belong in the wild. By letting them live freely, you're ensuring they're healthy, happy, and living life as they're meant to!

# OTTER FUN FACTS

You've already learned so much about otters, but there's still more to discover! Prepare to dive into a treasure trove of fascinating and delightful fun facts about otters.

Afterwards, test yourself in the quiz!

An otter's den is known as a holt or a lodge.

♡ ♡ ♡

Some otters have a pouch under their arms to store snacks and their favorite rocks.

♡ ♡ ♡

The sea otter can dive as deep as 330 feet in search of food. Although, this is quite rare.

♡ ♡ ♡

The giant otter, found in South America, can grow up to 6 feet in length!

♡ ♡ ♡

European Otters can stay underwater for up to 4 minutes.

The smallest otter, the Asian small-clawed otter, measures just about 2 feet from nose to tail tip.

♡ ♡ ♡

Otters have been found to use tools, especially sea otters that use rocks to crack open shellfish.

♡ ♡ ♡

Otters sleep holding hands to keep from drifting apart—a phenomenon called “rafting.”

♡ ♡ ♡

Their whiskers are super sensitive and help them detect the movements of their prey.

DESPITE THEIR PLAYFUL NATURE, OTTERS ARE FIERCE PROTECTORS OF THEIR TERRITORY AND CAN BE VERY VOCAL WHEN THREATENED.

Otters have a metabolic rate that's almost 3 times higher than ours; this means they eat a lot!

♡ ♡ ♡

Most otters have webbed feet, but the Asian small-clawed otter has only partial webbing because it handles more prey with its paws.

♡ ♡ ♡

Otters have been around for a long time—their ancestors date back 30 million years!

♡ ♡ ♡

A group of otters on land can be called a "romp," while a group in water might be called a "raft."

Otters' tails, called rudders, help them steer while swimming.

♡ ♡ ♡

The metabolic rate of sea otters slows down while diving, allowing them to stay submerged longer.

♡ ♡ ♡

Sea otters eat while floating on their backs, placing a "dining table" of kelp on their chests.

♡ ♡ ♡

The fur of the sea otter is denser than that of any other animal, with up to a million hair follicles per square inch.

OTTERS HAVE BEEN KNOWN TO PLAY WITH OTHER ANIMALS, LIKE SEALS AND EVEN DOGS!

A FEMALE OTTER'S GESTATION PERIOD (HOW LONG SHE IS PREGNANT)CAN VARY WIDELY, FROM 2 MONTHS TO A YEAR, DEPENDING ON THE SPECIES AND CONDITIONS.

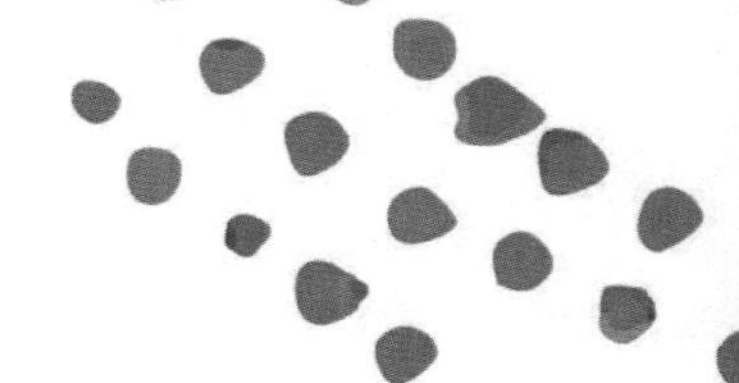

Otters can close off their ears and nose when underwater.

♡ ♡ ♡

Sea otters are considered a keystone species because their feeding habits help control sea urchin populations, which in turn allows kelp forests to flourish.

♡ ♡ ♡

In the wild, North American river otters can live up to 8–9 years, while sea otters can live up to 15–20 years.

♡ ♡ ♡

Even though sea otters live in saltwater, they have to come into freshwater areas to clean their fur.

Some species of otters are nocturnal, while others are diurnal.

♡ ♡ ♡

Otters have a very keen sense of smell and sharp eyesight.

♡ ♡ ♡

River otters can run on land as fast as 15 miles per hour!

♡ ♡ ♡

Otters have a strong, fishy-smelling breath due to their seafood-heavy diet.

♡ ♡ ♡

Asian small-clawed otters are known to form monogamous pairs that mate for life.

The oldest known otter fossil, Siamogale melilutra, was discovered in China and dates back 6.24 million years.

♡ ♡ ♡

The giant otter is known to have a unique throat pattern, which can be used to identify individuals, just like human fingerprints.

♡ ♡ ♡

Otters' hind feet are longer than their front feet, giving them added propulsion in water.

♡ ♡ ♡

An otter's tail makes up about a third of its body length.

DID YOU KNOW
THAT OTTERS'
SHARP CLAWS
HELP THEM
GRIP
SLIPPERY
FISH?

In cold waters, otters can raise their body temperature by increasing their metabolic rate.

♡ ♡ ♡

Otters have very flexible spines; this helps them twist and turn easily in the water.

♡ ♡ ♡

Otters have large lungs for their body size, which allow them to stay underwater for extended periods.

♡ ♡ ♡

Otters use their dung, known as "spraint," to mark their territory.

♡ ♡ ♡

There is a town in England called Ottery, which is on the River Otter.

Otters can move their nostrils and ears to be more streamlined while swimming at high speeds.

♡ ♡ ♡

The diet of an otter can change with the seasons, based on the availability of prey.

♡ ♡ ♡

Sea otters are one of the only marine animals to have fur instead of blubber to keep warm.

♡ ♡ ♡

Otters love to bask in the sun to dry off their fur, often seen lying on their backs on riverbanks or floating kelp beds.

OTTER FUR HAS A UNIQUE STRUCTURE, ALLOWING FOR AIR POCKETS THAT HELP IN BUOYANCY AND THERMAL INSULATION.

## WERE YOU PAYING ATTENTION?! TEST YOUR NEW OTTER KNOWLEDGE IN OUR QUIZ!

1. How many species of otters exist in the world?

2. Which otter species is known to hold hands while sleeping to stay together?

3. What type of water body does the sea otter primarily live in?

4. Describe one main difference between the European otter and the giant river otter.

5. Which part of the otter's body is especially adapted for efficient swimming?

6. What purpose do the otter's whiskers serve?

7. How do otters communicate danger to other members of their group?

8. Why are sea otters considered 'keystone species' in their ecosystems?

9. What is the primary diet of most otter species?

10. Which otter species is known for using tools, like rocks, to open shellfish?

11 In which part of the world can you find the festival dedicated to otters?

12 Why is it not recommended to keep otters as pets?

13 Name one threat facing otters due to human activities.

14 What is a significant cause of habitat loss for otters?

15 What are the dens or homes of freshwater otters called?

16 At what age do otter pups generally start to learn to swim?

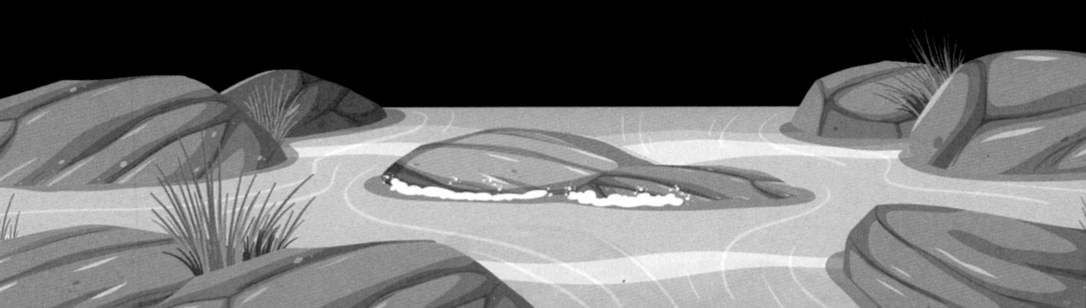

17 Where are otter babies, or pups, usually born?

18 How do otter mothers ensure their pups don't drift away when they go hunting?

19 How do young otters learn the skills necessary for hunting?

20 What is a male otter called?

# ANSWERS

1. 13
2. Sea otter
3. Ocean
4. Answers can vary. One main difference is European otters are generally more solitary and elusive. On the other hand, giant river otters are known for their social and family-oriented nature.
5. Webbed feet
6. Detecting prey and sensing their environment
7. Vocalizations or warning calls
8. Their feeding habits help control sea urchin populations, which in turn allows kelp forests to flourish.
9. Fish
10. Sea otter

11. Japan (Otter Festival in Kochi)
12. They have specific needs and thrive best in the wild
13. Pollution (or others like habitat destruction, hunting)
14. Urban development or damming of rivers
15. Holts
16. Around 2 months
17. Dens known as holts or lodges
18. Wrapping them in kelp or anchoring them
19. By imitating their mothers
20. Boar

# OTTERS
# WORD SEARCH

| | | | | | | | | | | | |
|---|---|---|---|---|---|---|---|---|---|---|---|
| F | D | C | R | A | F | T | Z | X | C | W | B |
| J | Q | D | S | I | V | H | G | F | D | H | G |
| F | L | O | A | T | V | Q | H | F | C | I | D |
| D | H | I | U | R | S | E | F | S | X | S | S |
| S | G | S | F | A | X | C | R | V | E | K | D |
| V | P | N | E | F | G | W | D | Z | J | E | F |
| C | M | L | C | A | R | N | I | V | O | R | E |
| X | J | D | A | E | O | M | N | X | B | S | Q |
| Z | H | F | Z | S | V | T | C | C | V | N | W |
| W | K | E | L | P | H | C | T | B | C | X | D |
| D | M | N | X | E | F | I | U | E | X | Z | S |
| F | W | E | B | B | E | D | V | C | R | X | C |

Can you find all the words below in the word search puzzle on the left?

**RIVER** **CARNIVORE** **FLOAT**

**KELP** **SEA OTTER** **SPLASH**

**WHISKERS** **WEBBED** **RAFT**

# SOLUTION

| | | | | | | | | | | | |
|---|---|---|---|---|---|---|---|---|---|---|---|
| | | | R | A | F | T | | | | W | |
| | | | | I | | | | | | H | |
| F | L | O | A | T | V | | | | | I | |
| | | | | | | E | | | | S | |
| S | | S | | | | | R | | | K | |
| | P | | E | | | | | | | E | |
| | | L | C | A | R | N | I | V | O | R | E |
| | | | A | | O | | | | | S | |
| | | | | S | | T | | | | | |
| | K | E | L | P | H | | T | | | | |
| | | | | | | | | E | | | |
| | W | E | B | B | E | D | | | R | | |

# SOURCES

"12 Facts About Otters For Sea Otter Awareness Week". (2017). Doi.Gov. https://www.doi.gov/blog/12-facts-about-otters-sea-otter-awareness-week.

"15 Fascinating Facts About Otters". (2023). Treehugger. https://www.treehugger.com/fascinating-facts-about-otters-4869357.

"18 Otter Facts From The Playful To Slightly Bizarre". (2023). TRVST. https://www.trvst.world/biodiversity/otter-facts/.

"All About Otters - Birth & Care Of Young| Seaworld Parks & Entertainment". (2023). Seaworld.Org. https://seaworld.org/animals/all-about/otters/care-of-young/.

BBC Natural History Unit. (2011). Otters: The Secret Life. BBC.

California Department of Fish and Wildlife. (n.d.). California's Wildlife: River Otters. Retrieved from California Department of Fish and Wildlife official website.

Duplaix, N. (1980). Observations on the ecology and behavior of the giant river otter Pteronura brasiliensis in Suriname. Revue d'Ecologie (Terre et Vie).

International Otter Survival Fund (IOSF). (n.d.). Retrieved from www.otter.org.

" IOSF ". (2023). Otter.Org. https://www.otter.org/Public/.

Kruuk, H. (2006). Otters: Ecology, Behaviour and Conservation. Oxford University Press.

Larivière, S., & Walton, L.R. (1998). Lontra canadensis. Mammalian Species, 587, 1-8.

National Geographic. (various dates). Various otter documentaries and episodes.

Reid, D.G., Code, T.E., Reid, A.C.H., & Herrero, S.M. (1987). Food habits of the river otter in a boreal ecosystem. Canadian Journal of Zoology, 65(6), 1308-1311.

U.S. Fish & Wildlife Service. (n.d.). North American river otter. Retrieved from U.S. Fish & Wildlife official website.

World Wildlife Fund (WWF). (n.d.). Otter. Retrieved from www.worldwildlife.org.

# You’re Otterly Fantastic!

As our delightful journey through the world of otters comes to an end, we hope you’ve enjoyed learning about these fascinating animals as much as we enjoyed sharing their story with you.

Your feedback means a lot to us, so we kindly ask you to leave a **review** on the platform where you purchased the book.

**Thank you for your support!**

## JOIN OUR VIP CLUB FOR FREE GIVEAWAYS AND MORE:

www.bellanovabooks.com/newsletter

# ALSO BY JENNY KELLETT

**... and more!**

Available at

www.bellanovabooks.com

and all major online bookstores.

Made in the USA
Middletown, DE
10 February 2024